Arthur
ASHE

ARTHUR ASHE
Tennis Great & Civil Rights Leader

by Chrös McDougall

ABDO
Publishing Company

Content Consultant:
Randy Walker, tennis historian

Published by ABDO Publishing Company, 8000 West 78th Street, Edina, Minnesota 55439. Copyright © 2011 by Abdo Consulting Group, Inc. International copyrights reserved in all countries. No part of this book may be reproduced in any form without written permission from the publisher. SportsZone™ is a trademark and logo of ABDO Publishing Company.

Printed in the United States of America,
North Mankato, Minnesota
112010
012011

 THIS BOOK CONTAINS AT LEAST 10% RECYCLED MATERIALS.

Editor: Rebecca Rowell
Copy Editor: Paula Lewis
Series Design: Christa Schneider
Cover Production: Christa Schneider
Interior Production: Christa Schneider

Library of Congress Cataloging-in-Publication Data
McDougall, Chrös.
  Arthur Ashe : tennis great and civil rights leader / by Chrös McDougall.
    p. cm. — (Legendary athletes)
  Includes bibliographical references and index.
  ISBN 978-1-61714-753-1
  1.   Ashe, Arthur—Juvenile literature. 2.   Tennis players—United States—Biography—Juvenile literature. 3.   African American tennis players—Biography—Juvenile literature. I. Title.
  GV994.A7M33 2011
  796.342092—dc22
  [B]
                         2010046583

TABLE OF CONTENTS

CHAPTER 1   **Wimbledon Champion**   6

CHAPTER 2   **Young Arthur**   16

CHAPTER 3   **Summers in Lynchburg**   24

CHAPTER 4   **College and the Army**   34

CHAPTER 5   **Going Pro**   44

CHAPTER 6   **South Africa**   54

CHAPTER 7   **Final Years of Tennis**   64

CHAPTER 8   **Embracing Retirement**   74

CHAPTER 9   **AIDS and a Legacy**   84

Timeline   96

Essential Facts   100

Glossary   102

Additional Resources   104

Source Notes   106

Index   110

About the Author   112

CHAPTER 1

Ashe makes a backhand return while playing Jimmy Connors in the men's singles final at Wimbledon in 1975.

Wimbledon Champion

Arthur Ashe Jr. was calm as he walked onto Centre Court at the All England Lawn Tennis Club on July 5, 1975. No black man had ever won the prestigious Wimbledon tennis tournament. And nobody thought Ashe would be the one to do it—not when facing Jimmy Connors, the best player in the world.

But challenges were nothing new to 31-year-old Ashe. He was used to people not expecting much of him as a tennis player. First, he was considered too small. Then, he was barred from tennis tournaments because he was black. When he finally started playing—and winning— tournaments, Ashe was mistaken for a waiter just as often as he was recognized as the man who had become a star black tennis player in a mostly white sport.

Sizing Up Connors

Those who wrote off Ashe's chances at Wimbledon in 1975 did so with good reason.

Grand Slams

Tennis has four major tournaments each year, which are called the Grand Slam events: the Australian Open, the French Open, Wimbledon, and the US Open. Only two male players have won all four tournaments in one year: Don Budge (1938) and Rod Laver (1962 and 1969).

Connors was nearly unstoppable. At 22 years old, he was the reigning champion in three of the four top tennis tournaments: Wimbledon, the Australian Open, and the US Open. Many thought he would have won the French Open as well—completing tennis's Grand Slam—but he had been barred from that tournament for playing World TeamTennis. Connors came to defend his title at Wimbledon as the tournament's top seed and the No. 1 player in the world.

Connors and Ashe were both from the United States, but that was all they had in common. Connors was brash, loud, and aggressive. Ashe was calm and graceful; he had been trained from a young age to control his emotions on the court. Connors, a dominant player, was known for intimidating his opponents with his powerful shots. Ashe, a finesse player, relied on consistent ground strokes. Ashe was a team player; Connors was not.

As Ashe walked onto Wimbledon's trademark grass court, he wore his blue Team USA jacket and two red-white-and-blue wristbands. He took great pride in representing his country, which he had done while in the army and in the Davis Cup, an international team tennis tournament. Connors, however, had refused to compete for Team USA in the Davis Cup. He also refused to join the Association of Tennis Professionals

Jimmy Connors

Jimmy Connors was a "bad boy" of tennis for two decades. He was known for his fiery personality, all-out playing style, and a dominant two-handed backhand. In 26 years as a pro, Connors won eight major singles tennis events, including the US Open five times. He is also the only player to win the US Open on three different surfaces: grass, clay, and hard court.

Born in 1952, Connors grew up in Belleville, Illinois, a city near St. Louis, Missouri. He learned tennis from his mother, grandmother, and a female teaching pro. Connors claims he first started playing tennis when he was two years old.

Connors broke onto the tennis scene when he turned pro in 1972, after spending one year in college. Although he was smaller than many of his opponents, Connors quickly established himself as one of the world's best tennis players. From July 1974 to August 1977, he was ranked No. 1 for 160 consecutive weeks. With 109 professional singles titles, he has won more than any other male player. In 1998, Connors was inducted into the International Tennis Hall of Fame.

(ATP), a players' union Ashe helped create to look out for the players' interests.

Tensions were naturally high between the two players, but they were heightened even more before this match. Earlier, Ashe had criticized Connors for not joining the ATP and called him "seemingly unpatriotic" for not competing in the Davis Cup.[1] On the night before their Wimbledon match, Connors announced he was suing Ashe for slander and libel.

The stage was set for Ashe to be embarrassed. As *Sports Illustrated* put it, Connors dominated his semifinal opponent so badly "that most people felt Ashe had no more chance than a scoop of ice cream in that fiery furnace."[2]

The Match

Ashe was known for his strong backhand and flat shots. At Wimbledon, he decided to attack Connors with his forehand and sliced, spinning shots. On the grass surface, these sliced shots would barely bounce. Connors would have to get low to return the shots, which meant his shots would have more arc and less accuracy. Ashe's tactic was called hitting junk balls. If he was nervous that day, he never showed it.

Ashe won the first set 6–1. The crowd was surprised, but onlookers were still not convinced Ashe could win. Ashe continued to feed Connors junk balls.

Connors put all he had into a forehand during his Wimbledon match against Ashe in 1975, but he simply could not defeat his fellow American.

"I remember being scared to death that Arthur was going to be totally embarrassed. We almost didn't want the match to happen because Connors was going to beat him 1, 1, and Love [6–1, 6–1, 6–0]. We were glad for Arthur that he got to the final, but we didn't even want to watch. But we had to."[3]

—*Bud Collins, commentator for NBC*

He knew Connors was at his best when hitting from the corners of the court, so he hit to the middle. Connors had a strong backhand return, so Ashe served to his forehand. Soon, Ashe was ahead 3–0 in the second set. Connors fought back, but to no avail. Ashe won the second set 6–1. He would need to win one more set to defeat Connors and become Wimbledon champion.

The fans in London, England, had embraced Ashe by the third set. Many had expected a boring match. After all, Connors usually dominated his opponents throughout the entire match. Now, fans could sense an upset, and in more ways than one. A black man might win Wimbledon.

Connors gained momentum in the third set, which he won 7–5. He celebrated with his trademark cheering and fist pumping after points. He quickly built a 3–0 lead in the fourth set. Ashe was at a crucial point in the match. He could change his game plan and go back to his strong shots, or he could continue hitting junk balls. Ashe stuck with his game plan, cutting Connors's lead. Soon, the fourth set was tied at 4–4. Then, Ashe took the lead and needed just one more game to win. At 40–15, match point, he served to Connors's backhand. The return floated back over the net to Ashe, and he slammed it back. Ashe had won Wimbledon.

After the awards ceremony, Ashe returned to the locker room. Neale Fraser, an Australian who had won Wimbledon in 1960, reached his hand out to Ashe. "Welcome to the club," he said.[4] Wimbledon had been played since 1877, and only 51 men had won the title, some of them more than once.

"I couldn't find an opening. . . . Everything he did was good: fine returns, short and long, and hard serves and volleys."[5]
—*Jimmy Connors, after losing to Ashe*

Ashe was the first black man to gain admittance to that elite group. It was an achievement he had spent his life preparing for and would spend the rest of his life using to benefit others.

Black Wimbledon Champions

As of 2010, Ashe remained the only black man to win Wimbledon. Three black women have won Wimbledon singles championships. Althea Gibson broke the color barrier at Wimbledon in 1951 and won the title in 1957 and 1958. Two black sisters from the United States would dominate Wimbledon 40 years later. Venus Williams won the tournament five times (2000, 2001, 2005, 2007, and 2008). Her sister, Serena Williams, won four times (2002, 2003, 2009, and 2010).

Ashe's 1975 Wimbledon victory was a personal and professional triumph as well as a step toward racial equality.

CHAPTER 2

The skyline of downtown Richmond, Virginia, Arthur's hometown

Young Arthur

Arthur Robert Ashe Jr. was born in Richmond, Virginia, on July 10, 1943. He was the first child of Arthur Ashe Sr. and Mattie Cunningham Ashe. When Arthur was only a few years old, the city hired his father to be a special policeman, assigned to oversee Brook Field, the largest blacks-only park in Richmond. The Ashe family moved into a single-story, five-bedroom house on Sledd Street, right in the middle of the park. Suddenly, Arthur was surrounded by basketball courts, baseball fields, and an Olympic-size swimming pool. And there were four tennis courts approximately 30 steps from his house.

Mattie taught her son, Arthur, to read as a toddler. By the time he was five, he was reading the daily newspaper. But his parents never allowed him to read comic books. He was a polite and obedient boy who went to church every Sunday. When Arthur was five, his brother, Johnnie, was born.

Segregated schools were common in the South, including Virginia.

It was a challenging life for the Ashe family. The parents tried to set a good example for their sons, but it was impossible to hide the fact that the boys did not have the same opportunities as whites. Virginia, like many southern states, was legally segregated. Laws required blacks and whites to use separate public facilities and services. Arthur was born in the city's blacks-only hospital, went to a blacks-only school, drank from blacks-only water fountains, and attended the blacks-only theater. The whites-only facilities were almost always better than those available to blacks. One blacks-only facility, however, Brook Field, would give Arthur the opportunity to change the world.

A Tragic Loss

In March 1950, Arthur's mother was hospitalized for minor surgery. After the procedure, Mattie Cunningham Ashe suffered from complications that worsened her condition. She died within a week. Arthur and Johnnie could have been sent to live with relatives. Instead, their father hired a housekeeper and took it upon himself to raise the two young boys. A strict father, he knew the boys would not get into trouble as long as he was in charge.

Growing up in Virginia could be dangerous for blacks. Many people still harbored attitudes of prejudice. Groups such as the Ku Klux Klan used violence in an attempt to enforce white supremacy. Arthur's father made sure his sons never put themselves into a situation that could lead to harm. Part of this involved keeping the boys close to home. When Arthur was in Baker Street Grammar School, his father timed how long it took him to walk home. After that, Arthur had to get home in

Family Tree

Arthur's cousin Thelma documented the history of the Ashe family in the United States in a giant family tree. Arthur's first documented ancestor was a slave from West Africa who arrived in Portsmouth, Virginia, in 1735. She was sold to a tobacco farmer and lived the rest of her life on his plantation. The ancestor, who was recorded only as "slave girl," eventually married a man on that plantation, and they had a daughter named Lucy.[1] Five generations of Ashe's ancestors would grow up in the United States before slavery was outlawed in 1865.

exactly that time every day or he would be punished. And his father never let Arthur have a job during his school years, though some other kids his age did. Instead, Arthur was responsible for chores around the house.

Discovering Tennis

A small and fragile boy, Arthur was often sick when he was young. Although he wanted to play football with the other boys at Brook Field, his father said no

Separate but Equal

The Thirteenth Amendment abolished slavery on December 6, 1865. But discrimination against blacks continued for many years, especially in the South. In the late 1880s, southern states began adopting Jim Crow laws, which called for blacks and whites to have separate public facilities and services. Some of these "separate but equal" laws pertained specifically to sports. For example, Georgia had a law regarding amateur baseball:

It shall be unlawful for any amateur white baseball team to play baseball on any vacant lot or baseball diamond within two blocks of a playground devoted to the Negro race, and it

shall be unlawful for any amateur colored baseball team to play baseball in any vacant lot or baseball diamond within two blocks of any playground devoted to the white race.[2]

Arthur experienced these laws while growing up in Richmond. When Arthur was eight, his cousin brought him to Sam Wood, an influential tennis director in Richmond. The boys asked Wood if Arthur could play in a tournament. "I would love to have you," Wood said. "But the time isn't right. The tennis patrons won't allow Negroes."[3] These Jim Crow laws were repealed in the 1950s and 1960s during the civil rights movement.

because of Arthur's size. Arthur tried swimming, but he was afraid of the water. So, he often played baseball, basketball, or tennis at Brook Field. He particularly enjoyed tennis.

Tennis was not popular among blacks during the 1940s and 1950s. The sport was mostly limited to rich white people and closed to blacks and lower-income whites. Most neighborhood boys Arthur's age preferred sports such as football or boxing. But something about tennis appealed to him. He started playing when he was six years old, although he often had no one to play with. Sometimes, he would watch the white boys play at Byrd Park, but it was illegal for blacks to play there.

One day, when he was nine or ten years old, Arthur watched 18-year-old Ronald Charity practicing his serve at Brook Field. It was the early 1950s, and Charity was one of the most accomplished black tennis players in Richmond. He was also a part-time tennis

American Tennis Association

When Arthur began playing tennis, the United States Lawn Tennis Association (USLTA) governed the sport for whites. Since blacks were not allowed to compete in USLTA tournaments, a group of blacks founded the American Tennis Association (ATA) in 1916 to govern the black game. The ATA was the first black sports organization in the United States. Although the sport remained segregated until the 1950s, the first interracial match took place in 1940 between Grand Slam winner Don Budge and ATA champion Jimmie McDaniel. Budge defeated McDaniel 6–1, 6–2 in an exhibition in New York before 2,000 fans.

instructor at Brook Field. When Charity saw Arthur, he asked the boy if he would like to join his tennis class.

Charity noticed that Arthur, although small, had good reflexes. Under Charity's guidance, Arthur became a respectable tennis player. Charity convinced Arthur to play in tennis tournaments. But no matter how talented, polite, and respectful he was, young Arthur was not allowed to play in white tournaments. At the time, he just figured that was part of life and tried to make the best of it.

Arthur received a high-quality tennis racket for his ninth birthday. As he continued to improve, he followed Charity to bigger tournaments throughout the area. But those days were numbered. One day in 1953, Charity took Arthur to Lynchburg, Virginia, to meet with Dr. Robert Walter Johnson. Arthur was confused. He did not understand why he was going to a doctor if he was not sick. As it turned out, the doctor wanted to watch Arthur play tennis.

Ron Charity

Ron Charity was an 18-year-old college student when Arthur first met him. Charity attended Virginia Union, an all-black school near Brook Field. Charity taught himself how to play tennis when he was 16 and went on to become a top player in Richmond. Despite his talent, Charity was barred from playing in many tennis tournaments because of his race.

Arthur later said that the years he spent with Charity "laid the foundation on which I built my career through the junior ranks, then as a college player and an adult amateur, then finally as a full-fledged professional."[4]

The tennis racket Arthur received for his ninth birthday would have been made of wood and quite different from those used by tennis players today.

CHAPTER 3

Tennis occupied much of Arthur's time after he moved to Lynchburg, Virginia.

Summers in Lynchburg

D r. Robert Walter Johnson was 54 when Arthur first met him. A successful black physician, Johnson had been a star athlete in his youth. He had dedicated the prior two decades to developing black tennis players who could succeed in the white-dominated sport. Johnson would select the most talented kids and train them at his home in Lynchburg, Virginia. He worked tirelessly to get his students entered into white tournaments. Because the window of opportunity was so small, Johnson did not take any chances. He trained only the best of the best, and he taught them to be disciplined on and off the court.

Arthur was only ten years old when he first met Johnson, and he had already picked up some bad tennis habits. Johnson had trained only teenagers and was not impressed with Arthur's size or natural talent. "He was the youngest in the group and so skinny he looked like he had rickets," Johnson said later.[1] But he also saw that Arthur

Getting in Trouble

When Arthur arrived in Lynchburg, Johnson's son tried to correct the player's backhand. But Arthur fought the change. "Mr. Charity showed me the other way," Arthur told him.[2] Johnson called Arthur's dad, who soon arrived in Lynchburg. He told Arthur that Johnson was trying to help him, and that if Arthur did not want to listen, he might as well go home. That was the last time Arthur got in trouble with Johnson.

was fast and worked hard. That summer in 1953, Johnson decided to take a chance and invited Arthur to Lynchburg.

Life with Johnson

Lynchburg was a three-hour bus ride from Richmond, and Arthur made the journey by himself. Johnson's large, three-story house was located in a neighborhood with both whites and blacks. The neighborhood was not like Arthur's. Johnson's house had a tennis court in the backyard, complete with a rebounding net and a ball machine. The court also had lights, which allowed Johnson and his students to play at night. Inside the house, Arthur had his own room upstairs. He shared a dressing room with three boys downstairs. Johnson paid most of the expenses, such as food and travel. It was a very different life than the one Arthur had been used to in Richmond.

If Arthur was looking for a break from the discipline his father instilled at home, he was not going to find it with Johnson. The boys had to wake up at 8:00 a.m., cook breakfast, clean their rooms, and be on the courts by 8:45. They would hit together all morning, have lunch, and then do drills. When not playing tennis, the boys had to do chores around the house, such as washing dishes or cleaning the doghouse, which was Arthur's least favorite task. Johnson also made sure the boys always dressed in their tennis whites. "[He] wanted us always to look immaculate and correctly dressed when we played, even for practice," Arthur wrote later.[3]

Johnson taught the boys to be polite and respectful on the court. He knew that black players would be scrutinized more closely than white players. Johnson even went so far as to have his students call any close shot in, just to avoid controversy. "If a ball landed slightly outside, we were to play it anyhow," Arthur wrote. "A reputation for sportsmanship was more important than a championship."[4] Arthur knew if he misbehaved on the court, his opportunities to play tennis could disappear.

Pancho Gonzales

Pancho Gonzales was one of Arthur's idols. Some consider Gonzales one of the best tennis players of all time. As a Mexican American, Gonzales was often an outsider at the white-dominated tennis tournaments. But he was fiercely competitive and won several major tennis events as an amateur. As a professional, he won the US national championship eight times between 1953 and 1961 and was ranked No. 1 in the world for eight years. Arthur admired Gonzales because, like himself, Gonzales was considered an underdog. Arthur was 11 when he first saw Gonzales play at a professional match in Richmond. Arthur was too nervous to ask for an autograph.

Becoming a Star Player

Arthur did not enjoy his first summer in Lynchburg. "The first summer was long, dull, and wearisome for me—especially since [Johnson] didn't enter me in any tournaments," he wrote later.[5] The boys would play tennis all day, and they would often talk about tennis or watch tennis footage with Johnson at night. It soon became clear to Arthur that he would need to continue improving under Johnson or he might not be invited back. So, he began to embrace the disciplined, hard-working lifestyle Johnson taught. He would spend more time on the court than anyone else and dedicate his time to studying strategies and tactics.

The hard work paid off. Soon, Arthur was thriving.

Johnson began taking Arthur to tournaments during his second summer at the tennis camp. Arthur often won his age group, though he was only able to compete in black-only American Tennis Association (ATA) tournaments. Two years later, he had a growth spurt and was no longer the smallest kid in the camp. As he grew, Arthur continued to find success and

"I remember the mandatory all-black schools, and the white line behind which I had to ride on buses."[6]
—*Arthur Ashe,* Days of Grace: A Memoir

break barriers on the tennis court. When he was 14, Arthur competed in his first biracial tournament and made it to the semifinals.

In 1958, Arthur entered the all-black Walker High School in Richmond. By that time, he was dedicating most of his time to tennis. In an effort to meet more people, he went out for the school's baseball and basketball teams. He also joined the school band, where he played trumpet. Although Arthur found success

Althea Gibson

Another successful tennis player emerged from Johnson's tennis camp. In the 1950s, Althea Gibson became the first black player to win at the Australian Open (doubles), the French Championships, Wimbledon, and the US Championships. In 1963, she became the first black to compete on the women's professional golf tour.

Born in Silver, South Carolina, in 1927, Gibson moved with her family to Harlem, New York, when she was three. Her family was poor, and Gibson hated school, but she loved sports. At age 12, she was the city's paddle-tennis champion. She then began playing tennis and won her first tournament at 14.

Gibson dropped out of high school and began focusing on the black-only ATA tournaments. In 1946, Johnson and another doctor, Hubert Eaton of North Carolina, took her in. She spent her summers with Johnson and winters with Eaton. Under their guidance, she not only became a top tennis player, but she also returned to high school, graduating in Wilmington, North Carolina, in 1949.

When she retired, Gibson had won 11 Grand Slam tournaments. In 1957, she was the first black to be named the Associated Press Female Athlete of the Year, an honor she won again in 1958.

in the other sports he played, he was forced to quit the baseball team because it had the same season as tennis. Even with all of his extracurricular activities, Arthur maintained good grades. He was also a star tennis player. Arthur continued to spend summers in Lynchburg, living and training with Johnson.

Competing in segregated Richmond had always been a challenge for Arthur. It only became more frustrating as the young tennis player became more skilled. He had been breaking color barriers and finding success in tournaments in other states. But he still was not allowed to compete against the top white players in Richmond, so his national ranking was not as high as it could have been.

In 1960, Arthur was finally allowed to play in the Mid-Atlantic Championship, a major tournament in the region. Just as he had done in many previous tournaments, Arthur became the first black player to win it.

Moving to St. Louis

After training for eight summers with Johnson, 1960 was Arthur's last year in Lynchburg. Before the teen's senior year in high school, Johnson had arranged for Arthur to move to St. Louis, Missouri, which was not segregated and afforded better competition in tennis. Although he wanted to stay in Richmond

Tennis took Arthur, *right*, to New York City in 1959, where he and Hubert Easton, *second from right*, played doubles in the Eastern Junior Tennis Championships.

and finish school with his friends, Arthur honored Johnson's wishes.

Arthur lived with Richard Hudlin, a black teacher, coach, and former college tennis star. As was the case with Johnson, Hudlin wanted to help other blacks succeed in tennis. While in St. Louis, Arthur played indoors on hardwood courts. The ball moved a lot faster on wood than it had on the clay courts Arthur played on in Virginia. He improved tremendously on

"While I was growing up, I was undoubtedly timid away from the tennis court. I was not only my father's child; I was wrapped in the cocoon of tennis early in life, mainly by blacks like my most powerful mentor, Dr. Robert Walter Johnson of Lynchburg, Virginia. They insisted that I be unfailingly polite on the court, unfalteringly calm and detached, so that whites could never accuse me of meanness. I learned well. I look at photographs of the skinny, frail, little black boy that I was in the early 1950s, and I see that I was my tennis racquet and my tennis racquet was me. It was my rod and my staff."[8]

—*Arthur Ashe,*
Days of Grace: A Memoir

the new courts, becoming a much faster player. In November 1960, Arthur won the national junior title. By the time he graduated from high school, Arthur was the fifth-ranked junior player in the nation.

Despite his success on the court, Arthur was often homesick in St. Louis. Hudlin was very strict, and Arthur did not have many friends. He graduated first in his class from Sumner High School in 1961, but he was glad when it was time to leave. "St. Louis was the worst nine months I ever spent," he wrote later.[7] However, he had a lot to look forward to. In the fall, he would attend the University of California–Los Angeles on a tennis scholarship.

Arthur moved to St. Louis, Missouri, as a teenager to better his chances of having a successful tennis career.

CHAPTER 4

The campus of UCLA

College and the Army

After graduating from high school, Ashe had his choice of several top colleges. Harvard University, the University of Michigan, Michigan State University, and the University of Arizona had all offered him tennis scholarships. The University of California–Los Angeles (UCLA) had as well. Arthur's father was wary of sending his son across the country for school, but he knew UCLA was a great opportunity. Beyond having one of the top tennis programs in the nation, UCLA was also known for its academics and for being open to black athletes. The Los Angeles area also offered year-round outdoor tennis and strong competition.

Ashe arrived in Los Angeles in 1961. He immediately liked and trusted his coach, J. D. Morgan. Though not a strict disciplinarian like Arthur's father or Johnson, Morgan did look out for Ashe. Los Angeles, especially the UCLA campus, was more welcoming to blacks than Richmond. But in his first year, Ashe was not invited to a major tournament in California because he was black. This frustrated him, but he chose not to challenge the decision.

Going to college so far from home—so far from segregation—opened Ashe's mind to many new people and new ways of thinking. He joined an all-black fraternity, Kappa Alpha Psi. He also enjoyed talking to all sorts of different people—black, white, or other—about the issues of the day. He had a part-time job taking care of the tennis courts on campus. And as a tennis player, Ashe was undefeated in his freshman year.

"There wasn't any doubt that UCLA would benefit my tennis more than any other school could."[1]
—*Arthur Ashe,*
Advantage Ashe

Wimbledon

In 1963, Ashe won the Southern California sectional title, which qualified him for Wimbledon. He wanted to go, but he was not sure if he could afford it. The cost of the trip to London, England, would be expensive. That April, after playing an exhibition match at a country club, a woman approached Ashe. She asked how much it would cost for him to fly to London to play in Wimbledon. When Ashe said $800, the woman left and then returned with eight $100 bills. She never told Ashe her name. Ashe was elated that he would now be able to compete outside the country for the first time—and it would be at tennis's most coveted event.

Ashe was fascinated by London. And he had a good tournament. He advanced to the third round before losing to Chuck McKinley. McKinley was the top-ranked US tennis player and went on to win the tournament. Ashe finished that summer ranked No. 6 in the country and was selected for the US Davis Cup team for the first time. The Davis Cup is an international team tennis tournament.

College athletes only have four years of sports

Black Athletes at UCLA

UCLA had a history of accepting black athletes before Ashe arrived on campus as the first black to receive a tennis scholarship to the university. Two prominent black athletes before Ashe were Jackie Robinson and Rafer Johnson. Robinson was a multisport star and a standout football player at UCLA. But he is best known for breaking the color barrier in baseball in 1947. Johnson won the gold medal in the decathlon at the 1960 Olympics in Rome, Italy. Prior to becoming an Olympian, Johnson was a star athlete and student body president at UCLA.

Ron Charity: Opponent and Partner

When Ashe was 15, he entered an ATA tournament in Norfolk, Virginia. One of his opponents was his old teacher, Ron Charity. He beat Charity for the first time. Defeating Charity bolstered his confidence. Ashe was not always Charity's opponent on the court. In 1961, before leaving for UCLA, Ashe teamed with Charity to win ATA's national doubles competition. It was Charity's only ATA national championship.

eligibility, regardless of when they graduate. Ashe finished his fourth year as the National Collegiate Athletic Association (NCAA) singles champion and captain of the NCAA champion team in 1965. He was an All-American for three of his four years at UCLA. After taking off the next semester, Ashe returned and graduated in 1966 with a bachelor's degree in business administration. He was the first person on his father's side of the family to graduate from college.

Joining the Military

When Ashe was at UCLA, all male students were required to participate for two years in the Reserve Officers' Training Corps (ROTC). The program teaches college students leadership skills and how to be an officer. Ashe decided to continue on that path, though it could have led to

Ashe won the National Clay Court Tournament in Milwaukee, Wisconsin, in July 1967.

him serving in Vietnam during the war (1954–1975). When he graduated from UCLA in 1966, Ashe went to Fort Lewis, Washington, for the summer. There, he continued training to be an army officer.

After basic training, Ashe enlisted at the United States Military Academy in West Point, New York. He earned the rank of second lieutenant and also served as an assistant tennis coach. Whenever possible, he competed in tournaments. And because he was representing his country, Ashe was also able to compete in the Davis Cup.

The US Open

In 1968, Ashe and the US team won the Davis Cup. It was the first of five consecutive wins. Later that year, he also won the national college championship representing UCLA. In March 1968, the International

The Open Era

Since tennis was an amateur sport when Ashe began winning tournaments, he was not paid. The sport changed in 1968 when the International Tennis Federation voted to allow amateurs and professionals to compete in the same tournaments. These events were called "open" tournaments.

Prior to 1968, most tennis players were amateurs. In the early history of the sport, many came from wealthy backgrounds and were supported by their country clubs, so prize money was not important. Until 1968, most major tennis tournaments were open only to amateurs. And although amateurs were not paid, many received money unofficially for competing.

As tennis became more popular, some top players turned professional to earn money for winning tournaments. These players could no longer compete in events such as Wimbledon. The first open tournament was the British Hard Courts at Bournemouth, England, in April 1968. Soon, nearly every top player turned professional and all top tournaments became open, including the Grand Slams. The US Open offered its first award of $14,000 to the men's singles champion in 1968, but Ashe could not accept it because of his amateur status. In 2010, both the men's and women's champions earned $1.7 million, with the potential for a bonus of up to $1 million.

Tennis Federation had approved of open tennis. This allowed tournaments to pay prize money and include professionals. That September, the first US Open was held, offering a $14,000 prize to the winner.

Because of his military commitments, Ashe was an amateur at the US Open and could not collect any prize money. He was given a small amount of money, $28 a day, for expenses. On September 9, after six rounds, Ashe—the fifth seed—found himself in the final against Tom Okker of the Netherlands. With his father and Johnson in the stands, Ashe defeated Okker to win the championship. The score was 14–12, 5–7, 6–3, 3–6, 6–3. He became the first black man to win a Grand Slam tournament. He later explained the importance of the event, writing:

Arthur Ashe Stadium

Nearly 30 years after Ashe's historic win at the US Open, the United States Tennis Association (USTA, formerly USLTA) opened Arthur Ashe Stadium in 1997 at the tournament's new location in Flushing, New York. This stadium is one of the premier tennis venues in the world and, with seating for approximately 23,000 fans, is also the largest. It serves as the main stadium at the USTA Billie Jean King National Tennis Center, where the US Open has been held since 1978.

The award ceremony that day will always hold a special place in my heart. My father came onto the court with me, and it felt wonderful to share that moment with him. Dr. J was in the stands.[2]

Although Ashe was not allowed to collect the prize money that day, he did receive the No. 1 world ranking among amateur players. Upon his return to West Point, his fellow cadets gave Ashe a three-and-a-half-minute standing ovation at dinner. And people around the world were now starting to take notice of Ashe. Soon, his popularity and career would skyrocket.

Ashe, *left*, celebrated winning the US Open men's singles championship with his father, who joined the tennis star on the court in September 1968.

CHAPTER 5

Throughout his life, Ashe shared his love of tennis with others. He often taught clinics to youngsters, including kids in Washington DC in 1968.

Going Pro

Top-level tennis changed forever when the open era began in 1968. The sport grew in popularity, helping players earn more money than they ever had before. Along with the influx of prize money at tournaments, professionals were also allowed to earn sponsorship money from companies.

In February 1969, Ashe completed his commitment to the US Army and was released from military service. Now 25 years old, Ashe decided to become a professional tennis player. He would compete in tournaments for prize money.

After Ashe turned professional, he began to sign endorsement contracts. Head, a sporting goods company, paid Ashe to use its rackets. Catalina paid him to wear its clothing. He also became a spokesman for Philip Morris and worked with companies such as Coca-Cola and American Express. With prize money and endorsements, Ashe would make more money than he ever had.

Playing for a Cause

The year Ashe turned pro, he also applied for his first travel visa to South Africa so he could play in the South African Open. Although Ashe was ranked the No. 1 player in the United States, he did not get that visa. As with other experiences during his childhood in segregated Richmond, Ashe was denied this opportunity because he was black. The South African government feared how people would react to having such a visible and successful black man visit the country.

While the United States struggled with race relations and segregation during the civil rights movement, South Africa was ruled by apartheid. During that time, people were strictly separated and given different privileges based on race. The native blacks of South Africa

Magazine Superstar

By the time Ashe turned professional, he had already been featured on the covers of major magazines, including *Life* and *Sports Illustrated*, and was profiled in the *New Yorker*. Growing up, Ashe had been featured in the *Sports Illustrated* "Faces In The Crowd," which recognizes up-and-coming athletes.

outnumbered the European colonists, but the white colonists controlled the country and had more privileges than South Africans of color. Ashe found this political system hypocritical and wanted to help change it.

Ashe committed himself to fighting apartheid and bringing attention to the cause. After being denied a visa in 1969, he decided to continue applying each year until South Africa granted his request. He also lobbied the International Tennis Federation and the Davis Cup

Taking a Stand

Throughout Ashe's career, he was often the first or only black competing in a given tournament. He often felt pressure from others and himself as a highly visible black athlete. For example, Ashe was expected to stay calm and to smile even when faced with insults. And as he became more famous, Ashe was increasingly expected to use his fame to help the black community. This sense of responsibility was heavy, especially during the civil rights movement of the 1960s, when blacks were fighting for equal rights.

Ashe's longtime lawyer, Donald Dell, remembered one incident in 1968 in Atlanta, Georgia, when some people were discussing the black movement:

A young guy yelled out, "Arthur, you've got to be more outspoken, more aggressive." And he said, "Jesse, I'm just not arrogant, and I ain't never going to be arrogant. I'm just going to do it my way."[1]

Ashe was not very comfortable speaking out on the issues when he was young. But he was a very thoughtful and inquisitive man. As Ashe continued to improve as a tennis player and mature as a man, he began to speak his mind more freely. Whether it was regarding black issues, tennis issues, or politics, he was not afraid to stand up against what he considered to be injustice.

to ban South Africa from their tournaments. In 1970, the Davis Cup did ban South Africa from competing.

Succeeding as a Professional Player

On the court, Ashe continued to succeed. He made the semifinals of Wimbledon and the US Open in 1969. Next, he made history in Australia. The amateur Australian national championships had opened up to both amateurs and professionals in 1969, becoming the Australian Open and the fourth Grand Slam event. The other major tennis tournaments—the French Open, the US Open, and Wimbledon—had already become open events. In 1970, at the second Australian Open, Ashe beat Dick Crealy of Australia in three sets: 6–4, 9–7, 6–2. Ashe became the first black to win the Australian Open singles title and the first non-Australian to win the title since 1959.

Ashe's tennis success continued into 1971, when he won the French Open men's doubles title with Marty Riessen. In other singles play, Ashe reached the semifinals of the US Open. And at Wimbledon that year, he made the doubles finals with Dennis Ralston. Ashe had become one of the top players in the world. He was also one of the more popular tennis players. As the only black player in the sport—and a very good player at that—Ashe, and the sport, continued to gain popularity in the early years of the open era. He became somewhat of a celebrity.

Players' Advocate

The sport's move into the open era brought a great deal of political posturing, as players, officials, and promoters all stood to profit from the new era of tennis. Fearful that the governing bodies and promoters would take advantage of the players, Ashe and others formed a union, the International Tennis Players Association (ITPA), in 1969 to protect players' rights.

Ashe served as treasurer for the original union. In 1972, the ITPA became the Association of Tennis Professionals (ATP). Ashe became its vice president.

Two of the ATP's principal values were that players should be paid fairly and should be able to choose which tournaments they competed in. The latter

Wimbledon 1969: Playing a Hero

In 1969, Ashe played his childhood hero, Pancho Gonzales, in the fourth round of Wimbledon. Ashe defeated Gonzales in four sets: 7–5, 4–6, 6–3, 6–3. Ashe won his next round match against Bob Lutz, but he lost to eventual champion Rod Laver in the semifinals.

Ashe in 1969, wearing his US Davis Cup uniform

was soon challenged. In 1973, a Yugoslavian player
named Nicola Pilic backed out of a commitment to
play on his country's Davis Cup team. In response,
the International Lawn Tennis Federation (ILTF)
banned Pilic from playing in any ILTF tournament for

30 days. That meant he would not be allowed to compete in Wimbledon, which was only a week away.

Since Pilic was a member of the ATP, Ashe and the players' union defended his right to choose not to play in the Davis Cup. The ATP leaders decided their players would not compete in any events during Pilic's 30-day suspension. The next day, most of the union's members backed the decision. If neither side budged, Ashe and many other top players would miss Wimbledon, one of the sport's premier events.

Ashe and the ATP collected signatures to show they were serious, but they also fought to get Pilic's suspension overturned so they could all play at Wimbledon. When the ILTF would not overturn Pilic's suspension, Ashe and other members of the ATP withdrew

Wimbledon Boycott

Tennis's premier event was spoiled in 1973 when 81 professional tennis players—mostly members of the ATP—boycotted Wimbledon. Among those were 13 of the top 16 seeds, including the 1972 champion, Stan Smith. The tournament went on with a strong women's field and a diluted men's field. Only two of the top ATP players competed. Ilie Nastase of Romania, who became the top seed, said his country forced him to play. Roger Taylor, Great Britain's best hope for a victory, was the third seed. In the end, second-seeded Jan Kodes of Czechoslovakia defeated non-ATP member Alexander Metreveli of the Soviet Union in the championship.

The ATP World Tour

In the late 1980s, the players thought tournament directors had too much power and the season was too long. At the 1988 US Open, the players held a press conference in a parking lot announcing they were backing the ATP to take over organization of the men's tour. The change was instituted in 1990, and what is now known as the ATP World Tour became the principal tennis tour for men.

from Wimbledon, including US player Stan Smith, the defending champion. It was painful for some of the world's top players to miss such an important tournament, but the ATP's boycott of Wimbledon eventually earned the players more freedom in determining their tennis schedules. In 1974, Ashe was elected president of the ATP. His advocacy for the rights of tennis players would continue. He would also branch out to show his support for other causes.

Ashe, *right*, and Davis Cup teammate Charles Pasarell enjoyed fishing in Australia in January 1969.

CHAPTER 6

South African heart surgeon Dr. Christiaan Barnard and Ashe, *right*, met at the Red Cross Children's Hospital in Cape Town, South Africa, in December 1973.

South Africa

In 1973, South Africa finally approved Ashe's request for a visa. He had been working to condemn apartheid and to get a visa since 1969. But now that he had been granted permission to visit the country, his decision to go was unpopular with a host of people.

Many critics believed the South African government approved Ashe's visa only to improve its image. If his visit went well, the country, which was still governed under discriminatory practices, might be seen in a more positive light. Due to widespread opposition to apartheid, South Africa had been banned from other major sporting events around the world, including the Olympics.

Some Americans wanted Ashe to focus on problems in his own country. Ashe, however, was adamant that the situation for blacks in South Africa was worse than it was for blacks in the United States. Under apartheid, blacks in South Africa were denied citizenship and had to live in one of four government-created homelands.

People could also be banned from society without a trial for disagreeing with apartheid.

As an athlete known around the world, Ashe believed he could help bring attention to the struggles of blacks in South Africa by going to the country. He wanted to use tennis to make a difference off the tennis court. If he went there to play and teach tennis, he might be able to visit with leaders and influence them. His goal was to observe as much as he could, talk to as

Apartheid

In 1948, the National Party gained control of South Africa's government. The party was composed of white descendants of Europeans, but most South Africans were not white. To better control the nonwhite majority, the National Party implemented apartheid laws to allow legalized segregation and discrimination based on race.

The apartheid laws divided people into four groups: black, colored (or mixed race), white, and Indian. The white minority then created rules to help whites stay in power and to keep the nonwhite majority under white control. Though they were vastly outnumbered, the whites took 80 percent of the land and did not allow nonwhites to enter without a pass. Nonwhites were limited to less-desirable jobs and forced to use separate, lower-quality public facilities. And some social interactions between the races were forbidden.

Nonwhites were strongly opposed to apartheid rule, but there was little they could do. Apartheid banned nonwhites from participation in the national government, stripping them of their South African citizenship. Few tried to publicly act against apartheid because the government could closely monitor them through a large network of informants. Those who were caught could be sent to jail or banned from society.

many people as possible, and then share his knowledge and experience with everyone who would listen.

Seeing South Africa

In November 1973, Ashe left for South Africa. After so much effort just to get into the country, Ashe made sure he was prepared when he got there. He spent hours reading about the nation and seeking advice from experts. He also set three conditions for his visit. Ashe would not play in front of a segregated audience. He would be labeled as a black man and not an "honorary white." And he would be free to go where he wanted and say what he wanted while there.

When Ashe arrived in Johannesburg, the largest city in South Africa, he immediately got to work. Frank Deford of *Sports Illustrated* was one of two journalists who accompanied Ashe on the trip. He wrote about how Ashe "solicited every possible view."[1] The tennis star met all kinds of people, including members of the government, the opposition, all races, clergy, journalists, businessmen, and sports figures.

"There is a concept in economics called comparative advantage, when two nations will trade with each other if they both believe they can gain. Now, I know the government is using me, but I'm using it, too."[2]

—*Arthur Ashe, on going to South Africa*

A non-Europeans-only bus in South Africa reminded Ashe of the segregation he and other blacks experienced in some areas of the United States.

Segregation was evident throughout the country. Most public facilities had signs announcing WHITES ONLY or NONWHITES ONLY. As was the case when Ashe was growing up in Richmond, Virginia, the separate facilities for blacks were much worse than those for whites. Ashe found that the blacks had terrible living conditions and had to take the hard, dirty jobs most people would likely not do if given a choice. The government forced the blacks who worked in Johannesburg to live outside the city in a neglected township called Soweto.

Ashe also learned that the government had a very strong presence in quieting dissenters. The Bureau of State Security, which was the government police, was everywhere. The press worried about being censored. Ashe said,

> It is amazing how few people realize what South Africa really is. It is a police state. The greatest, most influential variable here is fear. Wherever I go I see that everybody is afraid.[3]

As Ashe traveled around the country, he found many people open to and supportive of his visit. However, some South Africans disapproved. People whose views were on the far left generally opposed apartheid, but they opposed Ashe's visit because they felt he was making the government look good. People whose views were on the far right did not approve of Ashe's visit because he was breaking their segregation laws. And still others believed Ashe did not understand the country's problems and might be hurting the cause of anti-apartheid.

During one of Ashe's stops, he held a meeting with black journalists. They did not receive the tennis player well and accused him of being a "tool for the South African government."[4] The South African government might have planted informants at that meeting to make

Ashe look bad. Later, Ashe was confronted by blacks outside a tennis clinic who called him a "sellout and stooge."[5] Still, he carried on and tried to learn as much about the country and its people as possible.

South African Open

Despite the resentment from some, most South Africans held more moderate viewpoints and were excited about Ashe's visit. This was most evident at the South African Open. At Ellis Park, where the tournament was played, the fans had integrated seating for the first time. The formerly white section was filled with blacks. Ray Moore, a white South African tennis player, purposely sat in a section that had previously been blacks only. Even the locker rooms were integrated for the first time.

Nearly 100,000 people—a tournament record—came to

"I feel I have some credibility in talking about South Africa. I was brought up under a similar situation, having lived in the segregated South. I have more feeling being black, intuitively, than some northerner who may live with a false feeling of integration. . . . My first trip to South Africa convinced me that I could play a significant role as far as raising the level of awareness within the white community both in South Africa and the United States."[6]

—*Arthur Ashe,*
Off the Court

see Ashe play and most supported him. Ashe defeated South African Bob Hewitt in the quarterfinals and Cliff Drysdale in the semifinals. He lost to Connors in the finals. Ashe teamed with Tom Okker to win the doubles championship.

A Successful Trip

As Ashe had hoped, his public accounts of the horrors he saw in South Africa made many more people aware of the problems there. At the time, many athletes were competing in South Africa for large sums of money. Ashe continued to speak out against this and was successful in getting some athletes to change their minds. He also continued to encourage South African athletes to speak out against apartheid.

During his visit, Ashe showed many black South Africans that there was such

An Inspiration

Mark Mathabane is a black South African who was inspired as a boy by Ashe. Mathabane moved to the United States in 1978 to attend a US school with the help of a tennis scholarship. Later, he became a successful author. Mathabane described Ashe: "I [had] never seen a black man walk that proudly among whites. . . . One thing I found remarkable about Arthur Ashe was that he was not afraid to dismiss questions from white people if he considered them worth ignoring, and say what he considered important."[7]

Surprising Reaction

During his trip to South Africa, Ashe met with a professor at one of the nation's top universities. The professor was impressed that Ashe, a black man, was so well spoken. "You are an exception," he told Ashe. "You are not completely black; you have some white blood in you."[8] Ashe recalled being shocked that an educated man could believe apartheid was just and moral.

a thing as a free black man. On that trip, Ashe and Owen Williams, who ran professional tennis in South Africa, created the Black Tennis Foundation. The foundation worked to give every child in South Africa an opportunity to play tennis.

Although his initial trip brought more awareness of apartheid, it did not immediately lead to an end of the practice. Yet, his visit was a success personally and professionally. Ashe would visit the country repeatedly. As he continued to focus on the plight of black South Africans, he kept an eye on tennis as well.

Ashe made a forehand shot while playing Connors in the men's singles final of the South African Tennis Championships in Johannesburg in 1973.

Ashe, *right*, shook hands with Connors after defeating him in the men's singles final at Wimbledon in 1975.

Final Years of Tennis

Ashe's success as a professional tennis player continued into the mid-1970s. However, the 1975 Wimbledon victory would be Ashe's last major singles title. He would remain among the best players in the world for the next couple of years, but his Wimbledon championship would prove to be the peak of Ashe's tennis career.

According to Ashe, the beginning of the end of his career as a professional player came at the World Championship Tennis Finals in 1976. The 33-year-old Ashe was the top-seeded player in the tournament. But in the quarterfinals, he lost to the younger Harold Solomon. "It was a signal, which I tried hard to ignore, that I had passed my peak as an athlete," Ashe wrote.[1] Ashe went on to win the Australian Open men's doubles title with Tony Roche in January 1977, but he began to notice he simply could not keep up with his younger opponents.

Waiting to Marry

When Ashe was in his twenties, he decided to not marry until after he turned 30. Because of his tennis career, Ashe had a unique lifestyle in which he often traveled and met new people. "If I was going to give myself a chance to live out the dreams that I had when I was a kid reading all those *National Geographics* I couldn't get married," he wrote.[2] When he turned 30, Ashe consciously began to look more seriously for a wife.

Meeting His Wife

While Ashe realized his career as a professional tennis player was declining in 1976, his personal life was also changing. He found love. A strong supporter of the United Negro College Fund, Ashe was in New York City for a benefit on October 14, 1976. While there, he saw Jeanne Moutoussamy, a staff photographer assigned to cover the event for the television network NBC. Ashe thought she was beautiful, and after talking, they agreed to go on a date the next night. Ashe was so smitten after one date that he told his Aunt Marie that Moutoussamy might be the woman he would marry.

The couple continued dating for the next several weeks. Even though Ashe was often busy and traveling, he would call Moutoussamy every day. She was taken by his dedication.

Ashe and Moutoussamy on their wedding day

The two soon fell in love, and Ashe proposed a few weeks later. He put an engagement ring in an envelope and placed it in Moutoussamy's medicine cabinet. She found it three days later.

Ashe and Moutoussamy were married on February 20, 1977. Andrew Young, an ordained pastor and the US ambassador to the United Nations, performed the ceremony. Ashe had to attend on crutches because he had undergone foot surgery only ten days earlier.

Preparing for Retirement

The year 1977 started out well for Ashe, but his career suffered. His foot surgery and eye problems caused Ashe to miss most of the 1977 season, including three of the four Grand Slams. His world ranking fell from No. 2 in 1976 to No. 257 in 1977. Ashe struggled

United Negro College Fund

Ashe was a strong supporter of the United Negro College Fund (UNCF). The charity organization helps blacks pay for college and provides funds to the historically black colleges. In 2009, the organization provided operating funds to 39 schools and awarded 400 scholarships and internships to help low-income families better afford school.

Perhaps one of the reasons Ashe was so passionate about the UNCF is that he grew up across the street from a historically black college, Virginia Union University. Another school, Hampton Institute (now Hampton University), was also in the area. Ashe believed these schools helped preserve black culture in the United States. In his memoirs, Ashe wrote,

To this end, I am a veteran supporter of the United Negro College Fund. . . . I support the UNCF because of the high value I place on these colleges and because what they fund is both nonpolitical and highly efficient.[3]

The UNCF was founded in 1944 by Frederick D. Patterson, the president of the historically black college Tuskegee Institute (now Tuskegee University). The organization is based in Fairfax, Virginia.

with his confidence as he worked on his comeback for 1978. He was not sure if he could still keep up with the younger players. It set him back mentally when the clothing company Catalina decided not to sponsor Ashe after doing so for eight years.

But Ashe was able to overcome his doubts and made a strong comeback in 1978. By the end of the season, he had worked his way back up to No. 7 in the world, and ATP named him "Comeback Player of the Year." The 1979 season started slowly. For the second straight year, Ashe lost in the first round of Wimbledon. Unlike the season before, however, Ashe would not have a chance to redeem himself.

Health Scare

On July 30, 1979, Ashe awoke with terrible chest pains. Since he was an athletic, thin, nonsmoker and only 36 years old, he did not think it was anything serious. He figured it was indigestion and went back to sleep. Soon, he awoke again; the pain had increased. The pain came back a third time before it finally subsided and Ashe was able to fall asleep.

The next day, Ashe conducted two tennis clinics in New York City for underprivileged children. The pain returned. It had worsened, and it did not go away. A doctor who was on a nearby court came to Ashe and escorted him to New York Hospital. Ashe soon found

Ashe's Heart Attack

After Ashe was hospital- ized following his heart attack, many wondered how somebody as young and athletic as Ashe could suffer such an affliction. Heart attacks are more common in older people and among those who smoke and eat lots of fatty foods. But Ashe fit into neither of these groups. In his autobiography *Off the Court*, Ashe said a family history of hypertension and heart disease, as well as stress, likely caused his heart attack. Ashe's fitness might have been the reason he survived.

out that he had suffered a heart attack.

When Ashe was released from the hospital ten days later, he intended to return to tennis as soon as possible. Although he had done a lot in his career, Ashe felt he had more to do. His doctors were not so sure. They said he would have to undergo open-heart surgery if he were to return to the sport.

Six months later, on December 13, 1979, Ashe underwent a quadruple coronary bypass operation. Since the arteries in his heart were clogged, the doctors had to take veins out of Ashe's legs and use them to replace the clogged arteries in his heart. The surgery was successful, but the road to his return to tennis was just beginning.

In March 1980, Ashe was in Cairo, Egypt, with his wife and a friend, Doug Stein.

Ashe enjoyed the 1979 US Open as a spectator.

It had been three months since his surgery, and Ashe was feeling good and considered himself recovered. He had plans to return to professional tennis within weeks. But one day, Ashe was out for a run when he experienced angina, a painful feeling that occurs when the heart does not receive enough blood. He slowly walked back to the hotel, where he found his wife and Stein. Luckily, Stein was a doctor.

Stein assured Ashe it was not an emergency, but they decided to return to New York City as a precaution. Ashe wrote of the event, "As we flew out of Cairo, I knew one thing for sure: My career as a competitive tennis player was over."[4]

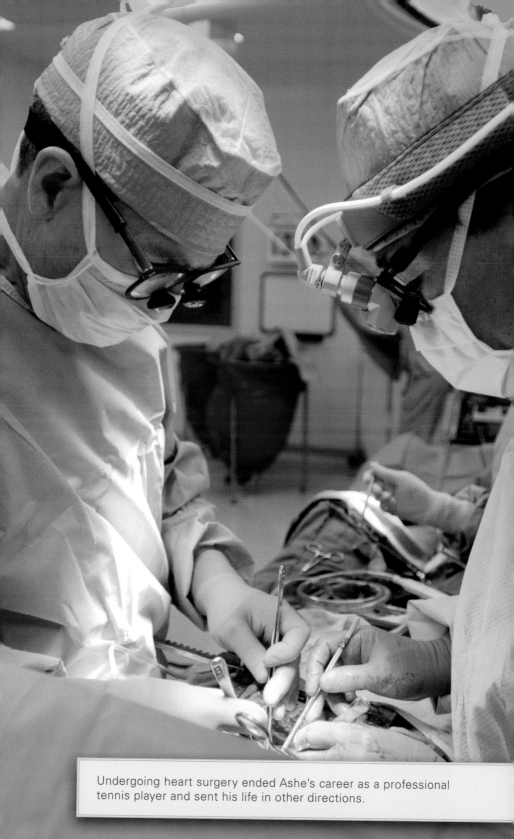

Undergoing heart surgery ended Ashe's career as a professional tennis player and sent his life in other directions.

CHAPTER 8

As US Davis Cup coach, Ashe, *center*, held the cup his team won in 1982.

Embracing Retirement

When Ashe could no longer meet the physical demands of playing professional tennis, he decided to leave the tour. He retired as a professional player on April 16, 1980. Retirement brought new possibilities to Ashe. He simply needed to decide what to do next. Through his tennis career and endorsements, Ashe did not have to worry much about money. He decided to use his fame to continue his work as an activist. He also wanted to stay involved in tennis.

Ashe wanted to be a public speaker. He also wanted to write, either for a book or a newspaper. He was interested in teaching as well. Ashe combined his interests and began writing a weekly tennis column for the *Washington Post*. He also occasionally wrote for *Time* and *Tennis* magazines. Soon, he became a television tennis commentator for ABC, HBO, and PBS. But his role with the US Davis Cup team was perhaps his most important and dearest to his heart.

Davis Cup Captain

When Ashe retired from playing professional tennis, he continued coaching at the Doral Resort and Country Club in Florida. He was not expecting to work with the Davis Cup team so soon. But in the summer of 1980, the United States Tennis Association (USTA) asked Ashe to captain the Davis Cup team. Unlike other sports, the captain did not actually play in the Davis Cup. Instead, the captain of the US team was in charge of selecting the players and setting the tone for the team. Ashe gladly accepted the offer and became Davis Cup captain in 1981. He brought his usual mindset to the role: Ashe wanted to win and to do so with class. He believed this was especially important while representing the United States.

The captain also needed to manage a variety of personalities, including some players with challenging egos. Ashe did not enjoy this aspect of the job. He struggled to find the right balance with the players. Some needed coaching and encouragement, while others despised it. Ashe, known for his

Dedicated to the Davis Cup

Proud to be an American, Ashe had wanted to represent the United States in the Davis Cup from a young age. Ashe first got that opportunity in 1963. At 20-years old, he was the first black to play on the US team. After playing his final Davis Cup match in 1978, Ashe's 27 Davis Cup singles wins were the most of any American at that point.

Ashe said of the Davis Cup, "It's nice to hear the announcer say 'Point—Ashe.' I'd rather hear 'Point—United States.'"[1]

calm demeanor, became upset with how some of his players acted on the court. Although he respected John McEnroe's dedication to the Davis Cup, Ashe struggled with McEnroe's fiery behavior. McEnroe and the newer generation of players were known for acting poorly on the court, often yelling and swearing at the referees, opponents, and fans. Team USA won the Davis Cup in 1981 and 1982, Ashe's first two years as captain, but lost in the first round of the Davis Cup in 1983.

Social and Political Activism

Ashe continued his social and political activism while serving as Davis Cup captain. He focused his efforts on many of the same issues he had throughout his career. In 1983, Ashe cofounded Artists and Athletes Against Apartheid to raise awareness for the cause and to encourage athletes and entertainers to boycott South Africa. Two years later, he was arrested for protesting apartheid outside the South African embassy in Washington DC.

While captaining the Davis Cup team in spring 1983, Ashe experienced heart trouble again. On June 21, the 39-year-old Ashe went back to the hospital for double bypass surgery on his heart. This surgery was harder on Ashe than his first surgery had been, four years earlier. Afterward, Ashe was still feeling weak. Doctors decided to give him a blood transfusion, a common procedure after a surgery to replace a patient's lost blood with blood from someone else. The transfusion helped. Although he had been depressed over the surgery and nearly resigned from the Davis Cup team, Ashe decided

Hall of Famer

In July 1985, just a few months before he resigned as Davis Cup captain, Ashe was inducted into the International Tennis Hall of Fame in Newport, Rhode Island. Athletes must have been retired for at least five years to be eligible. Ashe was inducted as soon as he was eligible.

against it. He continued his recovery and returned to his work as Davis Cup captain.

In 1984, Ashe convinced his old nemesis Jimmy Connors to join the team. With a star-studded lineup, the team made it to the finals before losing to Sweden. The team's behavior, however—namely that of McEnroe and Connors—was so offensive that the USTA started banning players from the Davis Cup tournaments unless they signed a contract saying they would behave in a sportsmanlike manner. Without McEnroe and Connors, who refused to sign the agreement, the US team lost in the 1985 quarterfinals. Ashe resigned as captain that October.

Becoming a Teacher

In 1985, Ashe was able to fulfill another goal for his retirement: teaching. He was offered a position teaching at Yale University, one of the most prestigious universities in the world. Instead, Ashe decided to take a position at Florida Memorial College (FMC), a small, historically black college near Doral, where he taught tennis. At FMC, Ashe taught an honors seminar called the Black Athlete in Contemporary Society.

Ashe, *left,* coached John McEnroe on the US Davis Cup team.

Ashe was an advocate for historically black colleges. He believed they preserved black culture and gave blacks opportunities they might not have had otherwise. When Ashe collected the first assignment, he was surprised to find that his students had very poor writing skills. Although he was a strong supporter of these institutions, Ashe was upset by the low standards set for black students. Although many of them came from rough backgrounds, Ashe pointed out that he had grown up in segregated Richmond and graduated from an all-black high school with straight As. He believed students would perform better if they were held to a higher standard.

This view led Ashe to speak out for higher academic standards for NCAA athletes. At the time, reports were surfacing about former college athletes who had been granted degrees but were only semiliterate. So the NCAA, which governs college sports, decided to raise the eligibility requirements for student athletes. Many people in the black community were upset. Because a lot of college athletes were black, opponents felt the changes were racist and would affect blacks more than any other group.

Ashe disagreed. He felt it was unfair that athletes were held to lower standards than other students who were also seeking scholarships. Although Ashe conceded that the new requirements might make it harder for blacks to get into college in the short term, he believed they would eventually meet the challenge. Ashe wrote essays for different publications supporting his view and got into disagreements with others in the black community over this issue. Even though blacks had been discriminated against in the past, Ashe did not believe in setting a lower standard for those of his race. He would continue to speak out.

Ashe's teaching job also introduced him to another cause. In preparing the syllabus for his class, Ashe was shocked to find only two books documenting blacks' history in sports in the United States. The most recent book had been published in 1948. Ashe knew he had the financial means and writing ability to document the history himself.

With his own money, Ashe and an assistant began collecting information about black athletes from any person or any source he could. It was a challenging task, and Ashe was sometimes depressed by the stories of great black athletes who were denied opportunities to compete because of their skin color. But he achieved his goal and documented all of those stories in a scholarly book for future generations. Ashe titled it

A Hard Road to Glory

Ashe spent approximately $300,000 of his own money to produce *A Hard Road to Glory: A History of the African-American Athlete*. The volumes have remained an important reference tool for the history of black athletes in the United States.

Throughout the process of developing the work, Ashe's biggest challenge was finding primary sources of information. Since blacks had not been considered full citizens for much of US history, there was not as much documentation of black athletes as there was for whites. Ashe and his assistant searched the country for any information they could find. They found some of the information in old newspapers and yearbooks, but much came from individuals who had saved mementos from previous generations.

Ashe found parts of the research to be challenging because many of the stories did not have happy endings due to discrimination the athletes had experienced. He also discovered many stories about great and popular athletes who had been forgotten by history. The *San Francisco Chronicle* called the series, "The most comprehensive reference source on African-American athletes yet compiled."[2]

Charitable Work

Ashe founded multiple charitable organizations. The Ashe-Bollettieri Cities Tennis Program was launched in 1988 as a tennis academy for inner-city kids. When funds dried up and Ashe's partner dropped out, Ashe created the Safe Passage Foundation to oversee the tennis program. He also created the Arthur Ashe Institute for Urban Health and the Athletes Career Connection to help black college athletes in their studies so they could graduate.

A Hard Road to Glory: A History of the African-American Athlete. The three-volume set was the definitive history of black athletes in the United States from 1619 to 1985. The books were published in 1988.

Becoming a Father

While Ashe was building careers in areas other than tennis, his personal life also took a new path. Ashe and his wife, Jeanne, had once considered not having any children. With histories of heart problems on both sides of the family, the couple worried their child would be vulnerable. However, they moved out of New York City after living there for almost 15 years and decided to have a baby. Camera Elizabeth Ashe was born on December 21, 1986.

Named after the equipment with which Jeanne had been so successful as a photographer, Camera was a healthy baby, to her parents' relief. Ashe embraced fatherhood. He also continued to stay involved in other commitments. But Ashe's health challenges would soon change in an unexpected way.

Ashe continued to teach children how to play tennis after he retired as a professional.

CHAPTER 9

Ashe, *right*, with his wife and daughter

AIDS and a Legacy

In the summer of 1988, while on vacation in upstate New York, Ashe wanted to make a telephone call. As he tried to push the buttons, he realized his fingers were not moving. Ashe was not very concerned. He thought it would go away. But his entire hand had soon turned numb. Ashe was able to see his doctor the next day.

The Diagnosis

The doctor determined something was blocking the nerve signals to Ashe's brain. Ashe underwent a series of tests, including a brain scan, to determine the cause of the blockage. After visiting various doctors, they concluded his only option was exploratory brain surgery. A few days later, Ashe went in for a series of preoperative tests, including a blood test.

The results of the blood test revealed Ashe had the human immunodeficiency virus (HIV). The brain operation confirmed the diagnosis of HIV. Soon, doctors discovered that Ashe had

AIDS

Doctors in the United States discovered cases of AIDS in 1981, approximately two years before Ashe was infected. The first case of HIV was discovered more than two decades earlier in Africa. As of 2010, doctors had made much progress with treatment options for HIV and AIDS. But there is still no cure. The deadly disease is present worldwide and is especially widespread in Africa. According to the United Nations, as much as 30 percent of some African nations' populations are infected. Many groups now work to promote AIDS awareness and prevention around the world.

Acquired Immune Deficiency Syndrome (AIDS), a condition caused by HIV.

HIV weakens the immune system, making it harder for a person to fight off disease. The virus is transmitted through body fluids. Since there is no cure, it ultimately leads to death. Many AIDS patients contract the disease through sexual activity or sharing needles while injecting drugs. Ashe's AIDS came from the blood transfusion he received after his second heart surgery. Ashe had lost a lot of blood during the operation and decided to have a transfusion rather than wait for his body to replenish itself naturally. Since AIDS had only recently been discovered at that time, hospitals had not yet begun testing the blood used for transfusions.

After the diagnosis, Ashe and his wife, Jeanne, decided to keep the news private. They would tell a few close friends but not Camera, who was only two years old.

AIDS was a misunderstood disease at the time with a stigma attached to it. If the public knew Ashe had AIDS, he felt his life as he knew it would change.

Ashe and Jeanne were relieved the news did not become public and that they did not have to explain to Camera that her father was sick. They were also relieved to learn that neither Jeanne nor Camera had been infected.

Ashe dedicated himself to privately fighting AIDS while continuing to be active in his political and business ventures. Although his health fluctuated, he generally felt okay.

Going Public

On Tuesday, April 7, 1992, everything changed for Ashe. He did not think much of it when his childhood friend Doug Smith stopped by for a visit. Smith was the tennis reporter for *USA Today*, and Ashe figured Smith just wanted to talk about *A Hard Road to Glory*. He was shocked when Smith asked if Ashe was HIV positive.

Somebody had sent a tip to *USA Today* that Ashe was infected with the disease. Although Smith was uncomfortable with the situation, it was his job as a journalist to try to confirm the rumor.

Ashe refused to confirm or deny the rumor and asked to speak to the paper's sports editor, Gene Policinski. He would have final say in whether the newspaper ran the story. Talking on the phone, Ashe and Policinski were immediately at odds. Ashe would not confirm or deny the rumor, but he did ask the newspaper to respect his privacy and not run the story. Policinski felt that, if true, the story should run in the next day's issue. Since Ashe was a public figure, Policinski thought the public had a right to know. Ashe was furious, arguing that he was no longer in the public spotlight since he had retired from tennis.

Negative Reaction

USA Today could not confirm the initial story about Ashe and did not run it. The newspaper did not have enough evidence before Ashe's press conference to verify he had AIDS. When Ashe was forced to announce his condition to the public, reactions to the newspaper's actions were mixed.

Many people agreed with Ashe that he was no longer a public figure and the public had no need to know of his condition. Hundreds wrote to the newspaper, and some canceled their subscriptions.

Those in the journalism community, however, tended to side with *USA Today*. Soon after the press conference, seven newspaper editors were polled while attending a convention in New York City. Of those seven, five said they would have run the story. The *New York Times* reported,

> They said Mr. Ashe's role as a barrier-breaking black tennis star, and his active involvement in an array of civil rights issues, made him a significant public figure. . . . That his disease was acquired immune deficiency syndrome, in itself a subject of great national importance, only added to the conviction of many editors that they would have published the news despite Mr. Ashe's wishes that it not be made public.[1]

When Ashe hung up the phone, he knew his secret would soon be revealed, even if *USA Today* could not confirm the story that night. If the public had to know of his condition, Ashe wanted to be the one to tell them. That night, he arranged a press conference for the following afternoon. Ashe then proceeded to call the people close to him who did not yet know. If *USA Today* broke the news the next morning, at least Ashe would be able to tell his friends first.

The Press Conference

The next morning, April 8, Ashe was surprised and relieved to find that *USA Today* had not run the story. Ashe could deliver the news himself. When he arrived at the press conference that afternoon, the room was filled with journalists. Ashe walked onto the stage with Jeanne, three doctors, his lawyer, and David Dinkins, the mayor of New York City.

Ashe read a prepared statement in which he explained how he had contracted the disease. He told the reporters the family kept the information private to maintain something of a normal life. When he went on to talk about Camera, Ashe began to cry. Jeanne stepped in and finished his thought. Ashe then explained what had happened with *USA Today* that forced him to reveal his secret. He did not blame the newspaper, knowing that *USA Today* was simply

Ashe composed himself during the news conference in which he announced he had AIDS.

doing its job. Regardless, he was still upset by what had happened.

When Ashe finished reading his three-page statement, he went on to answer questions. When asked about his future, Ashe said,

> I have been an activist on many issues in the past— against apartheid, for education and the athlete, the need for faster change in tennis. I will continue with those projects in progress, and certainly get involved with the AIDS crisis.[2]

After answering questions for 45 minutes, Ashe left the stage. His secret was out. It was time to move on.

Living Life to the Fullest

After announcing he had AIDS, Ashe tried living just as he had before the public knew of his affliction. He refused to ask his doctor how much longer he had to live. Instead, Ashe asked to be told when it was near so that he could be prepared. Until that day, Ashe tried to live every day to the fullest.

Ashe spent time with his family and friends. He had experienced some closure in his long fight against apartheid in South Africa when the government there repealed the final apartheid laws in 1991. Championing his other causes as well, Ashe created the Arthur Ashe Foundation for the Defeat of AIDS in 1992. And he spoke before the

Magic Johnson

About five months before Ashe's admission, basketball superstar Earvin "Magic" Johnson abruptly retired, announcing he was infected with HIV. Many considered Johnson to be the first major public figure to announce that he had HIV. His admission helped many people better understand the disease. "He is so known and loved," Ashe said, "that there was [an army] of doctors and articles explaining HIV transmission and treatments. You couldn't ask for better public education."[3]

United Nations General Assembly on World AIDS Day, encouraging more funds for AIDS research and stating how AIDS should be addressed globally.

In September 1992, Ashe participated in what would be his last protest. Opposing the US government's handling of Haitian refugees, Ashe and several hundred others marched on Washington DC. It was not a violent protest. The organizers told police exactly what they would be doing. But it was illegal to protest near the White House. Ashe and approximately 90 others were arrested that day. Ashe was held for about an hour before paying a small fine and returning to New York City. He suffered another heart attack the next morning, which might have been caused by the stress of being arrested. The heart attack was mild. Upon being released from the hospital, he quickly returned to his busy lifestyle.

During the fall of 1992, Ashe received many awards and recognition for his activism against AIDS and other causes, including the prestigious Sportsman of the Year award from *Sports Illustrated*. The magazine wrote about Ashe:

> Ashe always embodied good sportsmanship on the playing field. But if sportsmanship is also an athlete's ability to shift from being a selfish competitor to being a useful member of society, then Ashe's sportsmanship is unequaled. His gradual harvest has grown into a mountain of good.[4]

In late 1992, he founded the Arthur Ashe Institute for Urban Health. The organization worked to improve health care for urban minority populations. Ashe also spent some of his time finishing his memoir, *Days of Grace*. He completed it just before his death.

Remembering Ashe

Ashe died on February 6, 1993, at New York Hospital-Cornell Medical Center in Manhattan. The cause of death was AIDS-related pneumonia. He was 49 years old. His doctors were surprised that Ashe had lived more than four years after discovering he had AIDS in 1988. Although he had an incurable disease and his health had begun deteriorating about seven months earlier, those closest to him were still surprised when he did not recover from his latest illness.

Honored at Home

When Ashe was young, he would not have been allowed to visit Monument Avenue in Richmond. The road, which was lined with statues of Confederate army heroes, was only for whites. On July 10, 1996, however, on what would have been his fifty-third birthday, a statue of Ashe carrying a tennis racket in one hand and books in the other was added to Monument Avenue.

Newspapers and magazines nationwide ran glowing tributes to Ashe following his death. Friend and *New York Times* sports columnist William C. Rhoden wrote,

> *Arthur Ashe's impact—on our society, on the sociology of sports, on those he was close to—will be like a ripple on a pond, resonating from the center outward.*[5]

Ashe's body was taken to his hometown of Richmond, Virginia. A line of people—black and white—stretched for five blocks to pay their respects to Ashe as he lay in state in the governor's mansion. The last person to have that honor had been Confederate General Stonewall Jackson in 1863. Jackson had fought during the American Civil War to keep slavery. Now, the city that was once segregated was honoring one of its native sons, a black man.

"From what we get, we can make a living; what we give, however, makes a life."[6]

—*Arthur Ashe*

More than 6,000 people attended Ashe's funeral before he was buried at Woodland Cemetery in Richmond.

Ashe was recalled as a top tennis player, having won three singles Grand Slam titles and achieving the No. 1 world ranking—the only black man to do so. He was not the best player of his generation, but unlike most players, Ashe is remembered as a top tennis player who was also a world-renowned humanitarian.

USA 37

In 2005, the US Postal Service honored Ashe's memory with a stamp.

1943

Arthur Robert Ashe Jr. is born on July 10 in Richmond, Virginia.

1950

Ashe's mother dies in March.

ca. 1950

Ashe meets Ron Charity at Brook Field and begins to play tennis.

1961

Ashe moves to the West Coast and begins attending the University of California–Los Angeles on a tennis scholarship.

1963

Ashe plays in the Davis Cup for the first time.

1965

Ashe wins a collegiate national tennis championship and captains the championship team.

1953

Ashe spends his first of eight summers studying tennis with Dr. Robert Walter Johnson.

1960

Ashe moves to St. Louis, Missouri, for his senior year of high school to train with Richard Hudlin.

1961

Ashe graduates first in his class from Sumner High School.

1966–1968

Ashe attends the US Military Academy, where he earns the rank of second lieutenant.

1968

Ashe wins the US Open men's single title on September 9 and becomes the first black man to win a Grand Slam.

1969

Ashe completes his service in the US Army and becomes a professional tennis player.

TIMELINE

1969

Ashe helps found the International Tennis Players Association, which becomes the Association of Tennis Professionals in 1972.

1970

Ashe becomes the first black man to win the Australian Open men's singles title.

1975

On July 5, Ashe becomes the first black man to win the Wimbledon men's singles title.

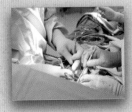

1983

After a second heart operation, Ashe receives blood carrying the HIV virus.

1985

Ashe is inducted into the International Tennis Hall of Fame in July; he resigns as captain of the Davis Cup in October.

1988

Ashe's three-volume history of black American athletes, *A Hard Road to Glory*, is published.

1979

Ashe suffers a heart attack on July 30; he has heart surgery on December 13.

1980

Ashe retires from tennis on April 16.

1981

Ashe becomes captain of the US Davis Cup team.

1988

Ashe is diagnosed with AIDS.

1992

Ashe holds a press conference on April 8 to announce he has AIDS.

1993

Ashe dies on February 6 as a result of AIDS-related pneumonia.

ARTHUR ASHE

ESSENTIAL FACTS

DATE OF BIRTH
July 10, 1943

PLACE OF BIRTH
Richmond, Virginia

DATE OF DEATH
February 6, 1993

PARENTS
Arthur Ashe Sr. and Mattie Cunningham Ashe

EDUCATION
Baker Street Grammar School
Walker High School
Sumner High School
University of California–Los Angeles

MARRIAGE
Jeanne Moutoussamy (1977)

CHILDREN
Camera Elizabeth Ashe

CAREER HIGHLIGHTS
Growing up, Arthur Ashe was a star while competing in American Tennis Association tournaments, which were mostly for blacks. In college, he became a national collegiate champion. Ashe won his first major tennis title, the US Open,

as an amateur in 1968. Two years later, as a professional, Ashe won the Australian Open. In 1972, he helped found the Association of Tennis Professionals (ATP). In 1975, Ashe became the first black man to win Wimbledon, one of tennis's most prestigious tournaments. After retiring in 1979, Ashe became the captain of the US Davis Cup team from 1981 until 1985.

SOCIETAL CONTRIBUTION

As a player, Ashe helped found the ATP to protect players' rights and traveled to South Africa to bring attention to apartheid. After retiring from tennis, he taught at Florida Memorial College and traveled the country speaking about his experiences. When he found no recorded comprehensive history of black athletes in the United States, Ashe took it upon himself to write it. *A Hard Road to Glory: A History of the African-American Athlete* was published in 1988. He created the Safe Passage Foundation to help black kids learn to play tennis and to do well in school. Later, after publicly admitting he had AIDS, Ashe created a foundation to help the fight against AIDS.

CONFLICTS

Growing up in Richmond, Virginia, Ashe experienced segregation. He was not allowed to go to the same school, play at the same parks, or play in the same tennis tournaments as whites. Later in his life, when Ashe became a celebrity, some blacks said he did not do enough to help the black community. One cause Ashe did take on was apartheid in South Africa. He spoke out against the practice for years and was arrested for protesting apartheid outside the South African embassy in Washington DC.

QUOTE

"From what we get, we can make a living; what we give, however, makes a life."—*Arthur Ashe*

GLOSSARY

activist
A person who supports or pursues a course of action involving a controversial issue.

All-American
An honor given to the best college athletes in a given sport.

angina
A severe chest pain caused by a lack of blood to the heart.

ball machine
An apparatus that serves tennis balls for practice.

basic training
Instruction for new military personnel.

cadet
A young person who is training to join the armed forces.

discrimination
Unfair treatment of a person or group based on prejudice about a given trait, such as race or religion.

endorsement
The public support of a product or company by an individual.

Grand Slam
One of the four major tennis tournaments: Australian Open, French Open, US Open, and Wimbledon.

humanitarian
A person who is committed to improving the lives of others.

hypertension
High blood pressure.

integration
When people of different races, ethnic groups, religions, genders, or social classes share the same opportunities.

pneumonia

A disease in which one or both lungs are inflamed, which causes difficulty in breathing.

refugee

A person who seeks protection from persecution by leaving his or her home country to live in another country.

segregation

The physical separation of people based on traits such as race, religion, or gender.

set

Part of a tennis match won by the player who wins six games first; sometimes more, because one must win by at least two games.

township

In South Africa, an urban, black-only settlement, often with lower-quality services than white areas.

visa

A document authorizing a person to enter a particular country.

white supremacy

The belief that the Caucasian race is superior to, and should rule over, all other races.

ADDITIONAL RESOURCES

SELECTED BIBLIOGRAPHY

Ashe, Arthur, and Neil Amdur. *Off the Court*. New York: New American Library, 1981. Print.

Ashe, Arthur, and Arnold Rampersad. *Days of Grace: A Memoir*. New York: Random House, 1993. Print.

Ashe Jr., Arthur, and Clifford George Gewecke Jr. *Advantage Ashe*. New York: Coward-McCann, 1967. Print.

Harris, Cecil, and Larryette Kyle-DeBose. *Charging the Net: History of Blacks in Tennis from Althea Gibson and Arthur Ashe to the Williams Sisters*. Chicago, IL: Ivan R. Dee, 2007. Print.

FURTHER READINGS

Benson, Michael. *Althea Gibson: Tennis Player*. New York: Ferguson, 2006. Print.

Djata, Sundiata A. *Blacks at the Net: Black Achievement in the History of Tennis*. Syracuse, NY: Syracuse UP, 2006. Print.

Steins, Richard. *Arthur Ashe: A Biography*. Westport, CT: Greenwood, 2005. Print.

Towle, Mike, Ed. *I Remember Arthur Ashe: Memories of a True Tennis Pioneer and Champion of Social Causes by the People Who Knew Him*. Nashville, TN: Cumberland House, 2001. Print.

LEGENDARY ATHLETES

WEB LINKS

To learn more about Arthur Ashe, visit ABDO Publishing Company online at **www.abdopublishing.com**. Web sites about Arthur Ashe are featured on our Book Links page. These links are routinely monitored and updated to provide the most current information available.

PLACES TO VISIT

International Tennis Hall of Fame Museum
194 Bellevue Avenue, Newport, RI 02840
401-849-3990
www.tennisfame.com
The museum chronicles more than eight centuries of tennis history within 18 galleries that include interactive exhibits, videos, and memorabilia.

United States Tennis Association Billie Jean King National Tennis Center
Flushing Meadows Corona Park, Flushing, NY 11368
718-760-6200
www.usta.com/About-USTA/National-Tennis-Center/
National%20Tennis%20Center/
The National Tennis Center, home to the US Open, is located in Flushing Meadows Corona Park. The Arthur Ashe Stadium is at the northern end of the park. Opened in 1997 and seating 23,000 fans, Arthur Ashe Stadium is the largest tennis stadium in the world.

SOURCE NOTES

CHAPTER 1. Wimbledon Champion

1. Arthur Ashe and Arnold Rampersad. *Days of Grace: A Memoir*. New York, NY: Random House, 1993. Print. 72.
2. Joe Jares. "A Centre Court Caste." *SI.com*. Time Warner, 14 July 1975. Web. 14 Oct. 2010.
3. Cecil Harris and Larryette Kyle-DeBose. *Charging the Net: History of Blacks in Tennis from Althea Gibson and Arthur Ashe to the Williams Sisters*. Chicago, IL: Ivan R. Dee, 2007. Print. 88.
4. Arthur Ashe and Neil Amdur. *Off the Court*. New York: New American Library, 1981. Print. 175.
5. "1975: Ashe's Wimbledon Win Makes History." *BBC Online*. BBC, 2008. Web. 14 Oct. 2010.

CHAPTER 2. Young Arthur

1. Arthur Ashe and Neil Amdur. *Off the Court*. New York: New American Library, 1981. Print. 16.
2. Vernellia R. Randall. "Examples of Jim Crow Laws." University of Dayton, 2001. Web. 15 Oct. 2010.
3. Arthur Ashe, Jr. and Clifford George Gewecke, Jr. *Advantage Ashe*. New York: Coward-McCann, 1967. Print. 19.
4. Arthur Ashe and Arnold Rampersad. *Days of Grace: A Memoir*. New York: Random House, 1993. Print. 60.

CHAPTER 3. Summers in Lynchburg

1. Frank Deford. "Service, But First A Smile." *SI.com*. Time Warner, 29 Aug. 1966. Web. 15 Oct. 2010.

2. Arthur Ashe and Neil Amdur. *Off the Court*. New York: New American Library, 1981. Print. 41.

3. Arthur Ashe, Jr. and Clifford George Gewecke, Jr. *Advantage Ashe*. New York: Coward-McCann, 1967. Print. 24.

4. Ibid. 41.

5. Ibid. 29.

6. Arthur Ashe and Arnold Rampersad. *Days of Grace: A Memoir*. New York: Random House, 1993. Print. 137.

7. Arthur Ashe, Jr. and Clifford George Gewecke, Jr. *Advantage Ashe*. New York: Coward-McCann, 1967. Print. 48.

8. Arthur Ashe and Arnold Rampersad. *Days of Grace: A Memoir*. New York: Random House, 1993. Print. 116.

CHAPTER 4. College and the Army

1. Arthur Ashe, Jr. and Clifford George Gewecke, Jr. *Advantage Ashe*. New York: Coward-McCann, 1967. Print. 50.

2. Cecil Harris and Larryette Kyle-DeBose. *Charging the Net: History of Blacks in Tennis from Althea Gibson and Arthur Ashe to the Williams Sisters*. Chicago, IL: Ivan R. Dee, 2007. Print. 97.

CHAPTER 5. Going Pro

1. Kenny Moore. "He Did All He Could." *SI.com*. 25 Feb. 1993. Web. 15 Oct. 2010.

CHAPTER 6. South Africa

1. Frank Deford. "Lull Beneath The Jacaranda Tree." *SI.com*. Time Warner, 10 Dec. 1973. Web. 15 Oct. 2010.
2. Ibid.
3. Ibid.
4. Arthur Ashe and Neil Amdur. *Off the Court*. New York: New American Library, 1981. Print. 154.
5. Ibid.
6. Arthur Ashe and Neil Amdur. *Off the Court*. New York: New American Library, 1981. Print. 148.
7. Sundiata A. Djata. *Blacks at the Net: Black Achievement in the History of Tennis*. Syracuse, NY: Syracuse UP, 2006. Print. 80.
8. Arthur Ashe and Neil Amdur. *Off the Court*. New York: New American Library, 1981. Print. 152.

CHAPTER 7. Final Years of Tennis

1. Ted Weissberg. *Arthur Ashe: Tennis Champion*. Los Angeles, CA: Holloway House, 1993. Print. 152.
2. Arthur Ashe and Neil Amdur. *Off the Court*. New York: New American Library, 1981. Print. 188.
3. Arthur Ashe and Arnold Rampersad. *Days of Grace: A Memoir*. New York: Random House, 1993. Print. 173.
4. Ibid. 36.

CHAPTER 8. Embracing Retirement

1. "Tennis: King Arthur." *Time.com*. Time, 20 Sept. 1968. Web. 8 Jan. 2010.

2. Arthur R. Ashe Jr. *A Hard Road to Glory: A History of the African-American Athlete: Basketball*. New York: Amistad, 1993. Print. Back cover.

CHAPTER 9. AIDS and a Legacy

1. Alex S. Jones. "Report of Ashe's Illness Raises an Old Issue for Editors." *New York Times*. 10 April 1992: A25. Print.

2. Arthur Ashe and Arnold Rampersad. *Days of Grace: A Memoir*. New York: Random House, 1993. Print. 17.

3. Kenny Moore. "The Eternal Example." *SI.com*. Time Warner, 21 Dec. 1992. Web. 15 Oct. 2010.

4. Ibid.

5. William C. Rhoden. "Arthur Ashe: A Hero in Word and Deed." *New York Times*. New York Times Company, 7 Feb. 1993. Web. 15 Oct. 2010.

6. "Puzzling." *SI.com*. Time Warner, 13 Oct. 2000. Web. 8 Jan. 2010.

INDEX

AIDS, 85–87, 88, 90–92, 93
All England Lawn Tennis
  Club, 7
American Tennis Association,
  21, 28
apartheid, 46–47, 55–56, 59,
  61, 62, 77, 90, 91
Arthur Ashe Foundation for
  the Defeat of AIDS, 91
Arthur Ashe Institute for
  Urban Health, 82, 93
Ashe, Arthur, Jr.
  arrest, 77
  birth, 17
  charitable work, 82
  Davis Cup captain, 75–78
  death, 93–94
  education, 19–20, 29–30, 32,
    35
  fatherhood, 82, 87
  health, 68, 69–70, 72, 77,
    82, 85–86, 87, 92
  military service, 38–39, 41,
    45
  retiring from tennis, 75, 88
  speaking out, 47
  teacher, 78–82
  wedding, 67
Ashe, Arthur, Sr. (father),
  17–20, 26, 32, 35, 38, 41–42
Ashe, Camera (daughter), 82,
  86–87, 89
Ashe, Johnnie (brother), 17, 19
Ashe, Mattie Cunningham
  (mother), 17, 19
Association of Tennis
  Professionals, 9–10, 49,
  51–52, 69

Athletes Career Connection, 82
Australian Open, 8, 29, 48, 65

Black Tennis Foundation, 62
Budge, Don, 8, 21

Collins, Bud, 12
Connors, Jimmy, 7–13, 61, 78,
Crealy, Dick, 48

Davis Cup, 9–10, 37, 40,
  47–48, 50–51
Days of Grace, 28, 32, 93
Deford, Frank, 57
Dell, Donald, 47
Drysdale, Cliff, 61

Florida Memorial College, 78
Fraser, Neale, 13
French Open, 8, 29, 48

Gibson, Althea, 14, 29
Gonzales, Pancho, 27, 49

Hard Road to Glory, A, 81,
  82, 87
Hewitt, Bob, 61
Hudlin, Richard, 31, 32

International Lawn Tennis
  Federation, 50–51
International Tennis
  Federation, 40, 47
International Tennis Hall of
  Fame, 9, 78
International Tennis Players
  Association, 49

Johnson, Earvin, 91
Johnson, Rafer, 37
Johnson, Robert Walter, 22,
  25–28, 29, 30–31, 32, 35, 41

Kodes, Jan, 51

Laver, Rod, 8, 49
Lutz, Bob, 49
Lynchburg, Virginia, 22,
  25–32

Mathabane, Mark, 61
McEnroe, John, 77–78
McKinley, Chuck, 37
Metreveli, Alexander, 51
Moore, Ray, 60
Morgan, J. D., 35
Moutoussamy, Jeanne (wife),
  66–67, 82, 86–87, 89

Nastase, Ilie, 51
National Collegiate Athletic
  Association, 38, 80

Okker, Tom, 41, 61

Pilic, Nicola, 50–51
Policinski, Gene, 87–88

Ralston, Dennis, 48
Reserve Officers' Training
  Corps, 38
Richmond, Virginia, 17, 20,
  21, 22, 26, 27, 29–30, 35, 46,
  58, 79, 93, 94
Riessen, Marty, 48
Robinson, Jackie, 37

Roche, Tony, 65

segregation, 18, 21, 36, 46, 56,
  58–59, 60
Smith, Doug, 87
Smith, Stan, 51, 52
South Africa, 46–48, 55–62,
  77, 91
Sports Illustrated, 10, 46, 57,
  92
Stein, Doug, 70
St. Louis, Missouri, 9, 30–32

Taylor, Roger, 51

United Negro College Fund,
  66, 68
United States Lawn Tennis
  Association, 21
United States Military
  Academy, 39
University of California–Los
  Angeles, 32, 35, 36, 37,
  38–39, 40
US Open, 8, 9, 29, 40–42, 48,
  52
USA Today, 87–89

Williams, Owen, 62
Williams, Serena, 14
Williams, Venus, 14
Wimbledon, 7–14, 29, 36–37,
  40, 48, 49, 51, 52, 65, 69
Wood, Sam, 20
Woodland Cemetery, 94

Young, Andrew, 67

ABOUT THE AUTHOR

Chrös McDougall is a sportswriter and an editor. As a sports reporter, he has covered a variety of events, from the Olympics to college football, basketball, and gymnastics. McDougall dedicates his first book to his grandparents, whose inspiration and support made it possible. He lives in Minnesota with his wife.

PHOTO CREDITS